Christı
Bible Skits

MW01491048

Written by
Shining Star Authors

Illustrated by
Don O'Connor

Cover Illustrated by
Janet Skiles

ISBN No. 0-7647-0502-4

To the Teacher/Parent

Christmas is probably the most popular time of year for children's pageants and programs. Unfortunately, there never seems to be enough time to organize and practice, so the final performances sometimes end up being less than perfect. It's true that this often makes a children's program more entertaining than if everything went according to plan. That's why most children's program directors have learned to have a philosophical attitude about the whole thing, realizing that parents are very undemanding about the level of excellence in the program if they can just get a good photo of their child in the spotlight.

This book is filled with a wonderful variety of simple, brief plays, skits, poems, and songs. They can be adapted to meet your needs and the number of children that need to be involved. The songs are simple but meaningful, and children will enjoy singing them. One of the best ways to help the children learn the songs is to have the church pianist play them as you sing them (or ask someone else to sing them) and record them on a cassette. Make duplicates of this music cassette for all the children to take home. Encourage parents to play the tapes in the family car and at home, perhaps when children go to bed at night. You'll be surprised at how much more quickly children learn the songs this way than if you tried to use just practice times to teach them.

Another suggestion is to ask some artistic people in your church to make simple costumes, props, and backgrounds for your performance. (Many costumes can be made using robes, towels, and rope.) Try to make the practices and performances enjoyable and meaningful experiences for your children (and for you, too).

Table of Contents

The Wise Men's Christmas

by Mary Tucker and Dorothy Penrice

Characters: a mixed-age group of church kids (six will have short speaking parts); Mr. B., the church janitor; pastor; children's choir (Use children's real names for character names.)

Setting: Children are in the church basement, helping the janitor clean.

Props: stacked chairs; boxes of Christmas decorations and costumes spilling over (including wise men costumes); cardboard star; bells the children can ring; cleaning tools, such as brooms, dusters, etc.

(All the children walk in from the back of the church, following Mr. B. to the stage, singing first song ("Come Celebrate Christmas," page 6). On stage, they finish the song and then begin to pick up things and clean.)

Child 1: What a mess! This will take us all day!

Mr. B.: Oh, it's not that bad. We just need to organize these things. You kids *(points to three children)* see what's in those boxes. *(Children begin going through boxes.)*

Child 2: Hey, look at the crazy costumes! *(pulling out an angel costume)*

Child 3: I remember that! My sister wore it when she was an angel in last year's Christmas play.

Child 4: *(puts on wise man's hat and robe)* Hey, look at me! I'm a wise man! *(puts arms out and struts around)*

Mr. B.: Wise guy is more like it!

Child 5: You know, I've always been kind of confused about the wise men. *(Other kids stop working to listen.)* Did they come to the stable to see baby Jesus or not?

Child 1: Sure they did! Haven't you read your Bible?

Mr. B.: Actually (kid's name), the wise men arrived in Bethlehem quite a bit later—maybe two years later. Jesus was a toddler by then, and He and His family were living in a house.

Child 4: The wise men should have taken the expressway—it would have got them there sooner.

Child 2: What *did* take them so long to get there?

Mr. B.: Well, you remember what made them go to Bethlehem, don't you?

Child 6: *(picks up cardboard star from the floor and holds it up)* The star!

Mr. B.: Right. Apparently that special star appeared in the sky when Jesus was born, but the wise men had a long distance to travel to get to Bethlehem. They somehow understood what the star meant, so they were willing to leave home and follow wherever it led them.

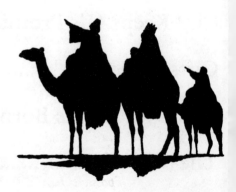

SONG: *All children sing "The Wise Men's Journey," page 7. Have three children sing the second verse as a trio, with the other children joining in on the chorus.*

Child 5: Isn't it interesting that the wise men followed the light of a star to find Jesus, the Light of the World?

Child 2: Hey, yeah!

The Wise Men's Christmas
continued

Mr. B.: That's a good point, (kid's name). God could have used any way He wanted to direct the wise men. Maybe He chose a star to guide them so we would be reminded that Jesus came to be the Light in a dark world.

SONG: *All children sing "Beautiful Star in the East," page 8.*

Child 1: What about those gifts they brought? They weren't exactly the kind of gifts most people would give a two-year-old.

Mr. B.: No, but maybe the wise men didn't know that the king they were going to see was only a baby.

Child 4: Sure, the Bible just says they were looking for a king. And their gifts were great for a king.

Pastor: *(walks in and greets children)* Hey, this is really nice of all of you to clean this place up! *(looks at child 4 who is still wearing the wise man costume)* Where's your camel (kid's name)? *(Children laugh.)*

Child 4: We were just talking about the wise men and how they came to see Jesus.

Child 3: Pastor, don't you think gold, incense, and myrrh were funny gifts to bring Jesus.

Pastor: Well, they didn't have *_____ back then you know. *(Children laugh.)* Actually, I think God was the one who made the wise men think of bringing those gifts.

Child 2: Why?

Pastor: Think about what happened after the wise men left.

Child 1: You mean when the angel told Joseph to get out of town because King Herod wanted to kill Jesus?

Pastor: Right. Joseph was a poor man. Where do you think he got enough money to take Mary and Jesus and live in Egypt for who knows how long?

Child 6: Of course—he sold the wise men's gifts!

Pastor: That's what a lot of Bible scholars believe. If that's what happened, it's clear that God was using the wise men to protect His Son.

Child 5: Wow!

Child 2: That's neat!

SONG: *All children sing "Wise, Wise Men," page 9.*

Pastor: I like that idea—that wise men still seek Jesus today. And Christmas is a great time for telling people about Him. Right?

All: Right!

Mr. B.: That's the best way I can think of to celebrate Christmas.

SONG: *All children sing first verse and chorus of "Come Celebrate Christmas," page 6. (If possible, have bells among props which children can ring for a big ending.)*

*Add whatever young child's toy is the most popular at the moment.

Come Celebrate Christmas
by Dorothy Penrice

1. Come cel - e - brate with us the birth - day of the King.
2. Man - y have ne - ver heard this bless - ed sto - ry true—

Ring out those Christ - mas bells, let ev - 'ry - bo - dy sing.
Jes - sus came down from heav - en just for me and you.

God's Christ - mas Gift has come, Je - sus the Fath - er's Son.
Born in a cat - tle stall, show - ing His love for all,

Let all the world re - joice, your wor - ship to Him bring.
That's why the Sav - ior came, the Fath - er's will to do.

Chorus

"Glo - ry to God" rang out that ear - ly Christ - mas morn.

Come cel - e - brate with us that Je - sus is born.

SS4861

The Wise Men's Journey
by Dorothy Penrice

1. We have seen that star in the sky— and it tells of the birth of the King. We must seek for Him, we must wor-ship Him, and our gifts to Him we'll bring.
2. We are tak-ing pre-cious gifts to Him— to this One, the ho-ly Son of God. We will seek un-til we have found this Child, then we'll wor-ship Christ the Lord.

Chorus

We are go-ing on a jour-ney. It may be ve-ry far. We will ride up-on our cam-els and fol-low that brill-iant star.

SS4861

Beautiful Star in the East
by Dorothy Penrice

1. Long, long a - go Ba - by Je - sus was born, born in a
2. When they ar - rived at the Beth - le - hem house, they found the

sta - ble so dim. God put a bright shin - ing
Child Je - sus there. Bow - ing be - fore Him they

star in the sky to guide the wise men to
gave Him their gifts, gifts that were prec - ious and

Him. Beau - ti - ful star, star in the
rare.

east, Bright - ly your beams shine in the night,

Lead - ing the wise men safe - ly to Him,

Safe - ly to Je - sus the Light.

SS4861

Wise, Wise Men

by Dorothy Penrice

1. How ve - ry wise were the wise men to foll - ow that bright star. They knew that a Ba - by King had been born; now they must tra - vel far. So night af - ter night they tra - velled, led by that brill - iant star un - til they came to Beth - le - hem and they found the young Child there.

2. Will you be like those wise men and seek the Sav - ior dear? No long - er is He in Beth - le - hem, but He is ve - ry near. He came to the earth from hea - ven, pre - cious and ho - ly One. And wise men still to - day seek Him, God's own dear be - lov - ed Son.

9

SS4861

'Twas the Fight Before Christmas
by Lisa D. Cowan

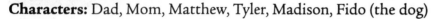

Characters: Dad, Mom, Matthew, Tyler, Madison, Fido (the dog)

Setting: a house

Props: To determine props, read through the rhyme and decide which setting you would most like to use. Gather props accordingly.

'Twas the fight before Christmas and all through the house
    not a creature was speaking; all were in the doghouse.

The stockings were hung from the chimney with care,
    but no happy faces could be found anywhere.

The children were sprawled out on top of their beds
    while echoes of "Gimme that" rang in their heads.

And Ma in her flannels and I in my ball cap
    had just about had it with the family's big spat.

When out on the lawn I did hear a faint patter,
    I got up from the couch to see what was the matter.

Away to the window, I walked cautiously
    And opened the vertical blinds so slowly.

The moon shone above the new fallen snow
    Giving hazy antiqueness to objects below.

Then what to my tired ole' eyes did appear,
    But a vision of the Christ Child with His family near.

With a glance at their surroundings of hay and of sticks,
    I decided immediately my family needed fixed.

More rapid than eagles, I flew up the stairs
    And whistled and shouted and called without flair,

"Hey Matthew! Hey Tyler! Hey Madison, too!
    Hey honey, come here, and yes, Fido, you, too!"

"To the top of the stairs, to the short landing wall
    Now everyone, everyone, everyone, ALL."

As the leaves that get stuck behind bushes and hedges
    Come trickling out with a rake's corner edges,

So to the staircase, the children all schlumped
    With their scowls and their frowns and their faces a-grump.

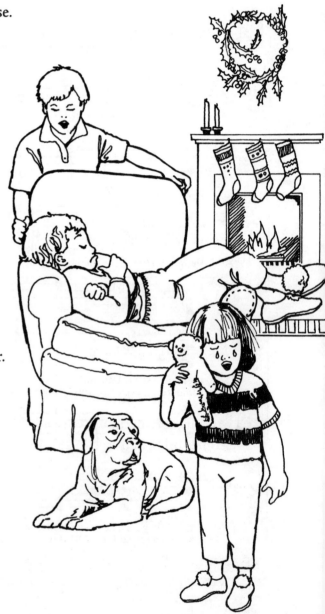

'Twas the Fight Before Christmas continued

And then with twinkling eyes, I did say,
"Children, now listen, tomorrow's a birthday.

"I've had it with video games, movies, and clothes.
I've had it with fighting about whose thing is whose.

"Our lives, mine included, are too much about things;
We've forgotten the joy that the Lord Jesus brings.

"It's His birthday tomorrow, not yours, yours, or yours,
And we've forgotten to choose a gift for our Lord.

"So ideas, ideas, we must think of one quick.
For His birthday's tomorrow, not silly St. Nick's."

Little Matthew spoke first, his face somber and sad,
"I think I have a gift, just a minute, Dad."

Then Matthew came back with his most favorite bear.
"Dad, how do we give Jesus somethin' . . . throw it up in the air?"

"No, no, my sweet Matthew, come on over, sit here.
To give to Jesus, we give to those who are near."

Then Tyler spoke up, "Hey Matt, what about Joy?
I bet she'd like him; she doesn't have many toys."

Matt hugged his dear bear, and over handed him,
"For Jesus' birthday, I guess I can give him."

Madison spoke not a word, but went straight to her room
And brought her Christmas dress of beige and maroon.

"There's a new girl at church. We've made fun of her clothes.
She comes on the church bus. I think her name's Rose."

Tyler sprang to his feet, to his dog gave a whistle.
They came back with his video, his or his sister's.

'Twas the cause of the spat on this very night.
He handed it over and said, "Sis, it's yours, alright."

Dad and Mom smiled, the kids smiled, too.
They needed this reminder of Christmas anew.

Dad then tucked the children in' bed for the night.
All were nestled and snug with hearts that were light.

But each heard Dad whisper as he climbed down the stairs,
"Merry Christmas, sweet Jesus! May Your love we share."

SS4861

The First Christmas
(A Play in Four Scenes)
by Anita Reith Stohs
Scene 1: An Angel Appears to Mary

Characters: narrator, Mary, Gabriel, rest of children (All)

Setting: Mary's home

Props: a simple chair, a rug, a small table, perhaps a bowl and spoon Mary could use to pretend to be cooking

(Option: The teacher can read the narration, and the class can be divided up to read the other two parts.)

Narrator: This morning, we are in Nazareth, a little town in the hills of Galilee. We are in the home of a young woman named Mary, recently engaged to a man named Joseph. Mary is busy at work, when suddenly she looks up in surprise.

All: Mary, Mary, what do you see?

Mary: An angel standing here by me.

Narrator: It is the angel Gabriel.

Gabriel: Greetings, Mary. The Lord is with you.

Mary: What is the angel doing here?

Narrator: Mary wondered.

Mary: What do these words mean?

Narrator: Mary was afraid.

Gabriel: Do not be afraid, Mary. You have found favor with God. You will have a baby. You will give Him the name Jesus. He will be great. He will be called the Son of God. God will give Him the throne of His father David. His kingdom will never end.

All: Mary, Mary, he says you're the one
To be the mother of God's own Son.

Narrator: Mary could not believe the angel's words. She asked the angel a question.

Mary: How can this be? I am not married.

Narrator: The angel answered her.

Gabriel: The Holy Spirit will come upon you. The baby will be the Son of God. Your cousin Elizabeth is also having a baby, though she is old. God can do anything.

Narrator: Mary answered the angel.

Mary: I am the servant of the Lord. May it be as you say.

The First Christmas
continued

All: Mary, Mary, what do you pray?

Mary: God's will be done with me this day.

SONG: *All children and Mary sing the words below. (Tune: Baa, Baa, Black Sheep")*

All: Mary, Mary what did you see?

Mary: The angel Gabriel there by me
With the news that I was chosen
To be the mother of God's Son.

All: Mary, Mary, what did you pray?

Mary: That God's will be done that day.

Scene 2: The Angel Appears to Joseph

Characters: narrator, Joseph, angel, Isaiah, rest of children (All)

Setting: Joseph's home, his bed (The angel appeared in his dream.)

Props: a bed or blankets to resemble one; a pillow

Narrator: Mary was engaged to a man named Joseph, but before they could be married, he found out that Mary was going to have a baby. The baby was God's Son, but Joseph did not know this.

Joseph: What am I going to do? Mary is going to have a baby, and it's not mine.

All: Joseph, Joseph, what will you do?

Joseph: I don't want people to make fun of her. I'll put an end to our engagement quietly. No one will know.

Narrator: But God has other plans.

All: Joseph, Joseph, God has good news.

Joseph: Before I could do anything, an angel of the Lord came to me in a dream. He called me by name, and I listened in amazement.

Angel: Joseph, son of David, don't be afraid to take Mary home as your wife. The baby is God's Son, through the power of the Holy Spirit. Mary will have a son, and you will call Him Jesus. He will save His people from their sins.

Narrator: All this happened to fulfill the words written long ago by the prophet Isaiah.

SS4861

The First Christmas continued

Isaiah: The virgin will be with child and will give birth to a son, and they will call him Immanuel—which means "God with us."

All: Joseph, Joseph, you now know what to do.

Narrator: When Joseph woke up, he did what the angel of the Lord had said. He took Mary home to be his wife and named the baby Jesus when He was born.

SONG: *All children sing the words below.*
(Tune: "Reuben, Reuben")

> Joseph, Joseph, what good news
> Mary will soon have a son.
> You will call the baby Jesus,
> He's God's Special Chosen One.

Scene 3: The Birth of Jesus

Characters: narrator, Joseph, Mary, rest of children (All)

Setting: the front of an inn; a stable

Props: a large box painted to look like an inn with a door cut in it, hay, a trough, a baby doll wrapped in a blanket

SONG: *All children sing "Clip, Clip, Clop" below. (Tune: "Three Blind Mice")*

> Clip, clip, clop.
> Clip, clip, clop.
> Mary rides,
> Mary rides
> A little donkey to Bethlehem town,
> Where Jesus the Savior is soon to be born
> In a stable with cows and sheep all around.
> Clip, clip, clop.
> Clip, clip, clop.

Narrator: It is late. All is quiet in Bethlehem town. But listen! Do you hear that?

All: Clip, clip, clop.

Narrator: A donkey is coming with someone on it. A man walks beside it. Who can they be that come so late? Where will they stay? It is the time of the emperor Caesar's census. There is no room in the inns in Bethlehem town.

14

SS4861

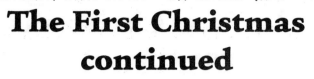

The First Christmas continued

All: Knock knock.

Joseph: Please, let us in. Please find a room for us in your inn. We need a place to stay. There is no room any other place in town.

All: No room. No room.

Joseph: But my wife is about to have a baby. Is there no way you can help us?

All: The stable, the stable. There is room in the stable.

Narrator: And so it was that Mary and Joseph came to stay in a Bethlehem stable, the home of the cows, donkeys, and sheep. There, during the deep, dark night, a little baby was born. Baby Jesus, the Savior of all, sleeps quietly in His manger bed.

Mary: Sleep, baby, sleep. You are wrapped all snug and tight in your warm clothes. Sleep quietly, snug and warm in the hay. Sleep, baby, sleep.

SONG: *All children sing "Sleep, Jesus, Sleep" below.*
(Tune: Three Blind Mice")

> Sleep, Jesus, sleep,
> Sleep, Jesus, sleep
> On Your bed of hay,
> On Your bed of hay.
> The stars are sparkling bright above
> While God, Your Father, looks down in love.
> You're the Prince of Peace that we all know of.
> Sleep, Jesus, sleep,
> Sleep, Jesus, sleep.

Scene 4: Angels Appear to the Shepherds

Characters: narrator, shepherds, angel, rest of children (All)

Setting: a field

Props: bright flashlights

Narrator: It is dark in the fields of Bethlehem. Shepherds sit by a fire close to their sleeping sheep. All of a sudden, the sky is filled with the glory of the Lord. *(Shine flashlights at shepherds.)*

The First Christmas
continued

Shepherds: We cannot see. The sky is filled with blinding light. What is happening?

All: Look up, shepherds. An angel comes with good news.

Angel: Don't be afraid. I have good news for you—news of great joy for all people. Today in the town of David, a Savior has been born. He is Christ the Lord. And this will be a sign. You will find the baby wrapped in cloths and lying in a manger.

All: Look up shepherds. Angels fill the sky.

Shepherds: Look at the sight. Listen to the song.

SONG: *All children sing "Glory to God" below. (Tune: "Jimmy Crack Corn")*

> Glory to God in the highest heaven,
> Glory to God in the highest heaven,
> Glory to God in the highest heaven
> And peace to men on earth.

Narrator: Then the angels left, and the sky was empty and still.

Shepherds: Did you hear what the angel said? The Christ has been born in Bethlehem. Let us go and see this thing that the Lord has told us about.

All: Go, go shepherds. Look for Christ the Lord.

Narrator: The shepherds ran to Bethlehem and found Mary, Joseph, and the baby lying in a manger. The shepherds spread the good news of Jesus' birth to all they met. And they returned to their sheep, giving God glory and praise.

SONG: *All children sing "Praise the Lord" below. (Tune: "Jimmy Crack Corn")*

> Praise the Lord in highest heaven,
> Praise the Lord in highest heaven,
> Praise the Lord in highest heaven
> For sending Christ the Lord.
>
> Spread the news of Jesus' love,
> Spread the news of Jesus' love,
> Spread the news of Jesus' love
> To everyone you meet.

SS4861

Baby Jesus
(Tune: "B-I-N-G-O")

This song is a lot of fun for children to sing on a variety of occasions.

There was a tiny baby boy
And Jesus was His na–ame,
J-E-S-U-S, J-E-S-U-S, J-E-S-U-S,
And Jesus was His name.

His mother sang Him lullabies
And Jesus was His na–ame,
J-E-S-U-S, J-E-S-U-S, J-E-S-U-S,
And Jesus was His name.

His father smiled at Him with pride,
And Jesus was His na–ame,
J-E-S-U-S, J-E-S-U-S, J-E-S-U-S,
And Jesus was His name.

He grew to be a loving child,
And Jesus was His na–ame,
J-E-S-U-S, J-E-S-U-S, J-E-S-U-S,
And Jesus was His name.

His birthday is on Christmas Day,
And Jesus is His na–ame,
J-E-S-U-S, J-E-S-U-S, J-E-S-U-S,
And Jesus was His name.

All shout: Merry Christmas, Jesus!

SS4861

Christmas Letters

by Jacqueline Schiff

Characters: 18 children

Setting: a classroom

Props: a chalkboard and chalk, a pointer; The chalkboard should be on the stage.

(Pairs of children walk on stage together and say their lines. After the second child in each pair says his or her line, the child writes his or her letter on the chalkboard. Then both children walk together to the rear of the stage. They stand there and wait.)

(First pair of children, taking center stage.)

Child 1: "C" for Christ Child, Heavenly King.

Child 2: "C" for carols people sing.

    (Child 2 writes capital letter "C" on chalkboard. Then both children walk together toward rear of stage.)

Child 3: "H" for harps the angels play.

Child 4: "H" for hymns of love and praise.

    (Child 4 writes capital letter "H" on chalkboard. Then both children walk together toward rear of stage.)

Child 5: "R" for riches the wise men leave.

Child 6: "R" for red poinsettia leaf.

    (Child 6 writes capital letter "R" on chalkboard. Then both children walk together toward rear of stage.)

Child 7: "I" for inn—no room to stay.

Child 8: "I" for innkeeper who turned a family away.

    (Child 8 writes capital letter "I" on chalkboard. Then both children walk together toward rear of stage.)

Child 9: "S" for star—the guiding light.

Child 10: "S" for shepherds who saw a great sight.

(Child 10 writes capital letter "S" on chalkboard. Then both children walk together toward rear of stage.)

Child 11: "T" for tunics—shepherds' clothes.

Child 12: "T" for tunes—flute music they chose.

(Child 12 writes capital letter "T" on chalkboard. Then both children walk together toward rear of stage.)

Child 13: "M" for manger where Jesus lay.

Child 14: "M" for magi from far away.

(Child 14 writes capital letter "M" on chalkboard. Then both children walk together toward rear of stage.)

Child 15: "A" for angels who came to say,

Child 16: "Alleluia! Christ is born today!"

(Child 16 writes capital letter "A" on chalkboard. Then both children walk together toward rear of stage.)

Child 17: "S" for stable filled with hay.

Child 18: "S" for Savior born that day.

(Child 18 writes capital letter "S" on chalkboard. Then the other children join child 17 and child 18, forming a line beside the board.)

All: *(together, as one child picks up the pointer and points to the letters as they are named)*

C-H-R-I-S-T-M-A-S spells Christmas!

(Child with pointer puts it down.)

All: *(together)*

Thank You, Son of God, above.
Jesus, Your name spells peace and love.

All: *(to audience)*

Merry Christmas, everyone.

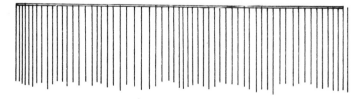

Music in the Stable

by Lois J. Zimmerman

Scene 1

Characters: narrator, Clara the cow, man in Biblical dress, woman in Biblical dress, donkey, 2 pigeons, 2 sheep, stable boy in Biblical dress, a group of singers (Animals may wear plastic headbands with appropriate ears attached and signs naming them.) (Note: Five additional characters appear in Scene 2.)

Setting: inside the stable with pigeons, sheep, and Clara the cow

Props: a cardboard box for manger, 2 mugs for milk

Narrator: It had been a cold day out in the pasture, and Clara the cow was glad to at last be in her stable. The straw was warm and clean with fresh straw in Clara's stall.

Clara was contentedly munching some fresh hay. *(Clara pretends to eat.)* She knew it was almost milking time, and the stable boy would be coming soon.

A noise at the door made Clara turn to look. Clara thought it was probably the stable boy and was surprised when she saw a man leading a small brown donkey. A woman was riding on the donkey's back. *(A man enters leading a donkey, and a woman is following slightly hidden behind donkey. The donkey hangs it head as if it is very tired.)*

The little donkey looked so tired—as if it had been traveling a long way. The woman smiled and patted the donkey *(woman smiles and pats donkey)* as the man helped her down from the donkey's back. *(Man helps woman.)*

The man put the donkey in a stall and gave him some grain to eat and a drink of water. *(Man leads donkey to make-believe stall and pretends to give it grain and drink.)* Then the man and woman sat down on a bed of fresh hay. *(Man and woman sit down on the floor.)*

Clara thought it was strange that the man and woman were staying in her stable. Surely they would be more comfortable in the inn. However, Clara did not know that all the inns in Bethlehem were full, and this was the only place left for the man and woman to stay.

SONG: "O Little Town of Bethlehem"

Narrator: The stable boy came and Clara gave him some milk. *(Stable boy enters and goes over beside Clara.)* He gave some milk to the man and woman before he left the stable. *(Stable boy gives two mugs to the man and woman and then he leaves.)*

Clara was happy to see how much the man and woman enjoyed the milk. *(Clara moos softly.)*

After they had finished the milk, the man and the woman settled down on their bed of hay to sleep. *(Man and woman lay down on the floor.)*

Music in the Stable
continued

The sounds of the stable were like comforting music. The pigeons cooed, the sheep baaed softly, the donkey occasionally brayed, and Clara added her low moo. *(All animals make appropriate sounds.)* Soon, all were asleep.

SONG: "Silent Night" *(first verse only)*

Scene 2

Characters: same as Scene 1 but add these: 3 shepherds in Biblical dress, 2 angels (may be dressed with just halos and wings or also with gowns)

Setting: same as Scene 1

Props: same as Scene 1 but add a baby doll wrapped in a white blanket

Narrator: Clara suddenly woke up. Goodness, it was so bright in the stable, and yet it did not seem like it should be morning!

Clara blinked her big brown eyes as she looked at the stable door. *(Clara moves head and looks toward the door.)* She saw that the bright light was coming from a brilliant star that hung low in the sky right above the stable.

(Three angels enter at this point.)

SONG: "Hark the Herald Angels Sing" *(first verse only)*

Narrator: There was the sound of angels singing, and then Clara heard a baby cry. Clara quickly looked toward the man and the woman. She saw that the woman was holding a newborn baby. The woman hummed a lullaby to the baby and called Him her sweet baby Jesus. She laid Him in the manger on a bed of sweet-smelling hay. *(Woman puts baby Jesus in a manger.)*

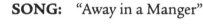

SONG: "Away in a Manger"

Narrator: Soon the shepherds came to the stable and knelt down to worship baby Jesus. *(Two shepherds enter and kneel in front of the manger.)*

Clara could not take her eyes away from baby Jesus and His happy parents. *(Clara looks toward baby Jesus and His parents.)*

(Shepherds exit.)

All the animals in the stable made their own special sounds, and Clara joined in with her low moos making joyful music for baby Jesus. *(All animals make their special sounds.)*

Clara's big brown eyes shone with love for she was very proud to share her stable with baby Jesus and His parents. This was a night that Clara would always remember.

SONG: "Joy to the World" *(first verse only)*

Heaven's View

by V. Louise Cunningham

Characters: angels—Celestial and Astral (they can wear white robes); Gabriel's voice; rest of children (All)

Setting: cloud workroom in heaven a few days before Jesus' birth

Props: cotton for clouds, bell

Celestial: Wasn't that meeting something special? I'm so glad that Galaxy was chosen to go to earth and sing to the shepherds. Aren't you glad I made you come before you finished fluffing up the clouds?

Astral: Thank you, Celestial. I wouldn't have missed it for anything. I wasn't sure any meeting was more important than fluffing clouds. I've seen how some go out of here, all flat and wispy.

Celestial: Can't you think of anything besides your clouds?

Astral: I can now. I'll never forget how Galaxy looked when her name was called to be in the angels' choir. She looked like an angel.

Celestial: She is an angel.

Astral: Of course, we all are. I forgot.

Celestial: Sometimes I think some of the air escapes from the clouds into your head. *(laughs)*

Astral: Michael looked so grand as he conducted the meeting. Everyone waited as still as the night for him to open the golden envelope to announce the angels' names.

Celestial: He said the Son of God could be born anytime.

(A bell is rung.)

Astral: There's the signal! It's going to happen now!

Celestial: It's about to begin. There goes Gabriel. Doesn't he look magnificent!

Astral: The sky is rolling back. I can see the shepherds!

Gabriel: *"Do not be afraid. I bring you good news of great joy that will be for all the people. Today in the town of David a Savior has been born to you; he is Christ the Lord. This will be a sign to you: You will find a baby wrapped in cloths and lying in a manger."* (Luke 2:10–12)

All: *"Glory to God in the highest, and on earth peace to men on whom his favor rests."* (Luke 2:14)

Celestial: Wasn't that heavenly? Those shepherds were really scared. Do you think they will go and find the baby? It doesn't look like they're moving.

Astral: Sure they'll go. They're just recovering from the shock. People aren't used to seeing angels.

SS4861

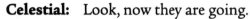

Celestial: Look, now they are going.

Astral: There's baby Jesus. But He's in a stable! The Son of God in a stable! That can't be right!

Celestial: It's too bad Mary and Joseph had to go to Bethlehem along with everyone else for the census. God planned it all. The Scriptures say Christ will be born in Bethlehem.

Astral: Of course, you're right. Look at how Mary is holding Him. She sure loves Him. *(pause)* She's not going to lay Him in the feeding trough!

Celestial: It seems full of straw. I heard that smells nice.

Astral: It wouldn't be as soft and fluffy as one of my clouds.

Celestial: Guess things are going as planned. The shepherds are at the stable door now.

Astral: How come Jesus wasn't born in a palace, and I thought wise men were supposed to come with presents? Think of all the Son of God gave up to live so humbly.

Celestial: God did it out of love for His people. I don't think we'll ever understand. Besides, if God had been born in a palace, do you think the servants would let those dirty-looking shepherds in to mess up the marble floors? Not on your life.

Astral: The shepherds are worshipping baby Jesus. I bet everyone will worship Christ the Lord.

Celestial: Somehow I have a feeling that won't happen.

Astral: Why wouldn't they after God has given them so much?

Celestial: God also gave man free will to make his own choices. The baby part appeals to a lot of people, but Jesus doesn't stay a baby. Most people aren't willing to accept the beliefs and teachings of God. We've seen in the past how prophets were rejected.

Astral: But God gave up heaven to go down there.

Celestial: I don't think that will matter to most people.

Astral: But for those who do make room for Jesus, it will be heavenly!

SONG: Children sing "There's Room in My Heart."

A Sharp Decision

by Connie Sorrell

Characters: narrator, Bobby, clerk, mother

Settings: Bobby's home, a store

Props: coins (in a piggy bank), slide whistle, triangle and stick, glock and stick, two pieces of sandpaper, sheet of paper, bell, box wrapped in Christmas paper

(This skit can be acted out or just read to the audience. Sound effects can be assigned to several children or just one or two.)

Narrator: It was the day before Christmas. Bobby took out his coin purse and counted his money. *(shake coins)* He only had $8.34 in his pocket. That was not enough money *(coins)* to buy his mother the new jacket that she wanted. Bobby said to himself,

Bobby: What can I do to earn some money quick? *(coins)*

Narrator: Bobby shook his head *(glock)* and pinched his nose *(triangle)* in deep thought. While he was thinking, he put his hand into his pocket and drew out his pocket knife. *(whistle)* It was a Swiss army knife. *(whistle)* Bobby really liked this one because it had three sharp blades, a toothpick, scissors, and a fingernail file. *(rub sandpaper)* Bobby said to himself,

Bobby: This knife *(whistle)* is worth a lot of money. *(coins)* I know what I can do!

Narrator: Quickly Bobby put the knife *(whistle)* back into his pocket. Then he went down to a local store where he had bought the knife. *(whistle)* Bobby walked *(glock)* to the service desk and spoke to the clerk.

Bobby: This knife *(whistle)* is like brand new. It is still very sharp. *(triangle)* Could I trade it in for the money *(coins)* that it is worth?

Narrator: The clerk looked at the knife *(whistle)* and then at Bobby. The clerk said,

Clerk: Do you have a sales receipt? Are you sure you bought it here?

Bobby: I don't have a sales receipt, but I am sure I bought it here.

Narrator: The clerk tapped *(triangle)* on the cash register then handed Bobby some money *(coins)* and took his pocket knife. *(whistle)* Bobby was sad to see it go, but he was glad to get the money. *(coins)* He walked *(glock)* over to the jackets and picked out a dark blue one that would fit his mother.

Bobby: This jacket will look so nice on my mother!

Narrator: After Bobby paid for the jacket, he hurried home and wrapped it in pretty Christmas paper *(wad paper)* and put a green bow on it. *(triangle)*

Bobby: Boy! What will Mother say when she sees what I got her!

Narrator: Early the next morning, Bobby was up and ready for Christmas time to start. He glanced at his four gifts, but he smiled *(bell)* at his mother's big gift. *(triangle)* That gift had cost him some money *(coins)* and his pocket knife *(whistle),* and it meant something to him. He give it to his mother right away.

Mother: Why, Bobby, what a big gift! You are so thoughtful!

Bobby: Hurry and open it! I know you will like it because it is what you wanted!

Narrator: Bobby's mother opened the gift. Her eyes became wet with tears.

Mother: Bobby, how could you afford such a nice jacket. You must have saved and saved your money. *(coins)*

Narrator: Bobby just smiled *(bell)* and kept his secret to himself. Now it was his turn to open his gifts. One gift was a new pair of pants and a shirt. Another was race cars, and another was the race track. He saved the littlest gift until last. When Bobby opened it, he was surprised.

Bobby: It's a nice leather pocket knife case! *(whistle)*

Mother: Now you can wear your pocket knife *(whistle)* on your belt, and it won't wear a hole in your pant's pocket. Get your knife *(whistle)* and try it out.

Narrator: Bobby didn't know how to tell his mother about his knife. *(whistle)* Would she be angry *(glock)* because he traded it for money *(coins)* or would she be pleased? *(triangle)*

Bobby: I don't have my knife *(whistle)* right now. I traded it for money *(coins)* so I could buy your jacket.

Narrator: Then Mother's eyes were really wet with tears as she hugged Bobby.

Mother: I know how much that knife *(whistle)* meant to you, Bobby. That makes my Christmas jacket even more special.

Narrator: Mother smiled. *(bell)* Bobby was glad he had given his knife *(whistle)* so Mother could have a warm jacket. It made him smile inside. *(bell and triangle)*

SS4861

Glory to God!
by Muriel Koller Larson

This is a wonderful song to sing at Christmastime to celebrate and remind others of Jesus' birth. To liven up the song, teach the children the motions to go with it.

Motions: "Glory to God" (Each time this is sung, throw hands upward.)

"He sent His Son to earth" (Bring right hand downward.)

"Praise the Lord for Jesus' birth" and "Praise Him for sending His Son" (Bring right hand upward.)

Suggested Program: Sing the chorus first, then ask the questions below and have the children give the answers.

> To whom should we give glory? (GOD)
>
> Whom should we praise? (GOD)
>
> Whom did God the Father send to earth? (OUR LORD JESUS CHRIST)
>
> Why did the Father send His Son Jesus? (HE LOVED US.)
>
> Why did our Lord Jesus come? (HE LOVED US.)
>
> What did Jesus do for us? (HE DIED ON THE CROSS FOR OUR SINS.)
>
> Is Jesus alive in heaven today? (YES! YES! YES!)

Now let's all say John 3:16 together: *"For God so loved the world that he gave his one and only Son, that whoever believes in him shall not perish but have eternal life."*

Sing the chorus again.

SS4861

Gifts

by Muriel Koller Larson

Sing this song to help the children learn all about the role the wise men played at Jesus' birth.

The wise men brought gifts to the Son of God. They came from a land a - far. They knew Je - sus was the King of Kings. They were led by God's bright star.

Chorus Gifts, gifts, gifts, God gave His Son for us. Gifts, gifts, gifts, What can we give to Him? Gifts, gifts, gifts, We'll give to God our love. Gifts, gifts, gifts, We'll al - ways live for Him.

Suggested Program: Sing the song, then ask the questions below, teaching the children the answers.

Who did the wise men know Jesus was? (THE KING OF KINGS)

What led them to Jesus? (GOD'S SPECIAL STAR)

What gift did God give us? (HIS SON)

What can we give the Lord? (OUR LOVE)

For whom should we live? (THE LORD)

SS4861

And the Angels Sang

by Lois J. Zimmerman

Scene 1

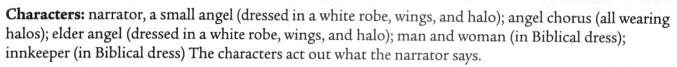

Characters: narrator, a small angel (dressed in a white robe, wings, and halo); angel chorus (all wearing halos); elder angel (dressed in a white robe, wings, and halo); man and woman (in Biblical dress); innkeeper (in Biblical dress) The characters act out what the narrator says.

Setting: heaven

Props: cotton, batting, or pillows for clouds; trumpet sound

(Sing as many verses of the Christmas songs as you want according to the length wanted for the program.)

Angel Chorus: *Sing "O Come All Ye Faithful."*

Narrator: The Small Angel had been waiting a long time for her first special assignment. She had heard some of the older angels talking about something special and wonderful happening on earth and how a large number of heavenly angels would have a special part in it.

The Small Angel was hoping she would be one of the ones chosen to take part in this special happening.

Suddenly, the Small Angel heard a trumpet blast *(trumpet sound)* that called the angels together for special assignments. She hurried to find her place to hear the announcements.

(Elder Angel enters, and the Small Angel stands near the Chorus of Angels.)

The wise Elder Angel of heaven began to tell the angels that a wonderful event was about to take place on earth. A special child was to be born, and an angel would announce His birth. Then a host of angels would sing praises to God. A group of shepherds watching their flocks of sheep would listen.

Angel Chorus: *Sing "It Came Upon a Midnight Clear."*

Narrator: The Elder Angel began reading the list of angel names that were going to sing in this special assignment. The Small Angel waited anxiously, hoping to hear her name. The list was almost finished, and just when the Small Angel had given up hope, her name, Rejoice, was read. To her joy, Rejoice was also chosen to announce the joyful news of the birth of the baby to the shepherds. Rejoice was so excited. She proudly took her place with the other special angels and listened to their directions.

(Small Angel, Rejoice, stands with Angel Chorus, and Elder Angel exits.)

And the Angels Sang
continued

The special angels were to be very near the earth and carefully watch two certain people. When the special baby had been born, Rejoice would announce the birth, and all the angels would sing above the field where the shepherds watched their sheep.

Rejoice watched closely as the man, leading a small donkey with a woman on its back, journeyed to the small town of Bethlehem.

(Man and woman enter to center stage.)

The man went from inn to inn looking for a place to stay, but every inn was full.

(Innkeeper enters and stands near man and woman.)

At the last inn, the kindly innkeeper offered the man and woman a clean stable where they could spend the night.

(Innkeeper exits.)

Angel Chorus: *Sing "O Little Town of Bethlehem."*

Scene 2

Characters: same as Scene 1 but no elder angel or innkeeper; add three shepherds (in Biblical dress)

Setting: man and woman with manger and baby *(center stage)*, shepherds to one side of stage

Props: box for a manger; a baby doll wrapped in a blanket; spotlight, if available

Narrator: During the night, a bright star hovered over that stable, and a special baby boy was born.

(Use a spotlight if available.)

In a loud clear voice, Rejoice told the shepherds of the baby's birth. The host of angels began to sing, "Glory to God in the highest, and on earth peace to men on whom his favor rests."

Angel Chorus: *Sing "Hark the Herald Angels Sing."*

(Shepherds kneel before the manger. Rejoice stands beside the manger.)

Narrator: The Small Angel, Rejoice, sang louder and more beautifully than any other angel. She was so happy to be part of this special night when baby Jesus was born.

All: *Sing "Joy to the World."*

Christmas Lambs
by Edith E. Cutting

Have the children sing the action song below to the tune of "Itsy Bitsy Spider." They may be dressed in white to represent lambs, or they could have white baby blankets around their shoulders.

Song	Actions
We were little lambs	*(Put hand to chest to identify self.)*
By Bethlehem that night.	
Angels came and sang	*(Raise arms toward heaven.)*
Out from a shining light.	
Shepherds were afraid,	*(Shudder or cover face with hands.)*
But we kept still and heard	
A voice from out the skies	*(One hand at ear, as if listening)*
More clear than any bird.	
"Fear not, I am with you,"	*(Quotation may be a solo.)*
The angel sang with joy.	*(Hands down, eyes raised)*
"Go now to Bethlehem;	
You'll find a baby boy.	*(Cradle arms and look down as if at baby.)*
He is the Christ	
Who is born to save us all."	
The shepherds left us here	
And followed up the call.	*(Point off-stage.)*
Baby Jesus grew in	
Love both wide and deep.	*(Stretch out arms.)*
He called people to Him	*(Arms beckon.)*
As if they were His sheep.	
We are all His children	*(Hands to chest for self-identification again)*
Who follow where He trod.	
We are His lambs	
And He's the Lamb of God.	*(Arms raised)*

A Trip Back to Christmas Past

by Jacqueline Schiff

Characters: 10 travelers who travel back in time to celebrate the first Christmas; Children portraying travelers may read their lines because some parts are more complex.

Setting: stage

Props: children's lines

Traveler 1: *(taking center stage)*
I went to the Mideast
And who did I meet?
Shepherds kneeling
At an infant's feet.
(Traveler 1 moves to rear of stage.)

Traveler 2: *(taking center stage)*
I went to the Mideast
And who did I meet?
Shepherds kneeling
At an infant's feet,
And pilgrims visiting
A child so sweet.
(Traveler 2 moves to rear of stage.)

Traveler 3: *(taking center stage)*
I went to the Mideast
And who did I meet?
Shepherds kneeling
At an infant's feet,
And pilgrims visiting
A child so sweet,
And Mary and Joseph
By the fire's heat.
(Traveler 3 moves to rear of stage.)

Traveler 4: *(taking center stage)*
I went to the Mideast
And who did I meet?
Shepherds kneeling
At an infant's feet,
And pilgrims visiting
A child so sweet,
And Mary and Joseph
By the fire's heat,
And mules and cattle
And bleating sheep.
(Traveler 4 moves to rear of stage.)

Traveler 5: *(taking center stage)*
I went to the Mideast
And who did I meet?
Shepherds kneeling
At an infant's feet,
And pilgrims visiting
A child so sweet,
And Mary and Joseph
By the fire's heat,
And mules and cattle
And bleating sheep,
And baby Jesus
Warm, fed, and asleep.
(Traveler 5 moves to rear of stage.)

Traveler 6: *(taking center stage)*
I went to the Mideast
And who did I meet?
Shepherds kneeling
At an infant's feet,
And pilgrims visiting
A child so sweet,
And Mary and Joseph
By the fire's heat,
And mules and cattle
And bleating sheep,
And baby Jesus
Warm, fed, and asleep,
And angels singing
As the joyful weep.
(Traveler 6 moves to rear of stage.)

SS4861

A Trip Back to Christmas Past continued

Traveler 7: *(taking center stage)*
I went to the Mideast
And who did I meet?
Shepherds kneeling
At an infant's feet,
And pilgrims visiting
A child so sweet,
And Mary and Joseph
By the fire's heat,
And mules and cattle
And bleating sheep,
And baby Jesus
Warm, fed, and asleep,
And angels singing
As the joyful weep,
And an innkeeper listening
Without a peep.
(Traveler 7 moves to rear of stage.)

Traveler 8: *(taking center stage)*
I went to the Mideast
And who did I meet?
Shepherds kneeling
At an infant's feet,
And pilgrims visiting
A child so sweet,
And Mary and Joseph
By the fire's heat,
And mules and cattle
And bleating sheep,
And baby Jesus
Warm, fed, and asleep,
And angels singing
As the joyful weep,
And an innkeeper listening
Without a peep,
And wise men bringing gifts
For Jesus to keep.
(Traveler 8 moves to rear of stage.)

Traveler 9: *(taking center stage)*
I went to the Mideast
And who did I meet?
Shepherds kneeling
At an infant's feet,
And pilgrims visiting

A child so sweet,
And Mary and Joseph
By the fire's heat,
And mules and cattle
And bleating sheep,
And baby Jesus
Warm, fed, and asleep,
And angels singing
As the joyful weep,
And an innkeeper listening
Without a peep,
And wise men bringing gifts
For Jesus to keep,
And Simeon living
For the child he'd meet.
(Traveler 9 moves to rear of stage.)

Traveler 10: *(taking center stage)*
I went to the Mideast
And who did I meet?
Shepherds kneeling
At an infant's feet,
And pilgrims visiting
A child so sweet,
And Mary and Joseph
By the fire's heat,
And mules and cattle
And bleating sheep,
And baby Jesus
Warm, fed, and asleep,
And angels singing
As the joyful weep,
And an innkeeper listening
Without a peep,
And wise men bringing gifts
For Jesus to keep,
And Simeon living
For the child he'd meet,
And nine other travelers
Spending Christmas with me.
(Traveler 10 stays in place. Other players join him or her on center stage.)

All Ten: *(joining hands)* Merry Christmas!

God Keeps His Promises
by Dorothy Penrice

Characters: narrator (this can be a child or the teacher), Joseph, 8 children to read "Promises" poem (below)

Narrator: Promises, promises! All of us make promises. But do we always keep our promises? Unfortunately, no. The wonderful Christmas story reminds us again that God always keeps His promises. Long before Jesus was born in Bethlehem, God had promised He would send Jesus to the earth to be our Savior. The first promise that He would send a Savior is found in the first book of the Bible— Genesis. Isaiah tells us that Jesus would be born of a virgin and His name would be Immanuel. He also said *"For to us a child is born, to us a son is given . . ."* (Isaiah 9:6) The prophet Micah even tells us he would be born in Bethlehem. As we will see, God kept all of these promises. We can always count on God.

All: *Sing "You Can Always Count on God," page 36.*

8 Kids: *Recite P-R-O-M-I-S-E-S poem below by Linda Penrice.*

P is for a Promise
The angel gave one day.
Mary would have a baby,
So Gabriel did say.

R is for Redeemer;
God would send His Son
Down to earth from heaven
To die for everyone.

O will stand for Only
God's begotten Son.
He was born a Baby,
Yet the Eternal One.

M is for gentle Mary.
At first she never knew
She would watch Him die one day—
Die for her sins, too.

I is for Isaiah,
A prophet of long ago.
He said this baby would be born,
And it happened just so.

S is for Simeon.
In the temple, he did pray
To see the Messiah with his eyes.
What a special day!

E is for everlasting—
The life God promises me.
If I trust Him as my Savior,
From sin, He'll set me free.

S is for the Savior
Promised long ago.
God always keeps His promises—
The Bible tells me so.

SS4861

God Keeps His Promises
continued

Narrator: The Christmas story starts not in Bethlehem, but in Nazareth. An angel sent by God appeared to Mary and told her she would be the mother of the promised Savior. The angel also came to Joseph, to whom Mary was engaged, and told him this amazing news.

Joseph: One night while I was sleeping,
An angel came to me
And brought a message right from God.
"Fear not, fear not," said he.
I should take Mary for my wife
And she would bear God's Son.
His name is to be Jesus,
For He will save from sin.

Narrator: Joseph and Mary were married, and just before Jesus was born, they had to travel to Bethlehem to be taxed, according to the decree of Caesar Augustus. Of course, when they arrived in Bethlehem, the town was so crowded with people who also had to be taxed, they were unable to find any place to stay. Because it was time for Jesus to be born, they were thankful for an innkeeper who allowed them to stay in his stable.

All: *Sing "There's Room in the Stable," pages 37–38.*

Narrator: And so it was, that Jesus was born in an innkeeper's stable. The Bible says that Mary wrapped Him in swaddling clothes and laid Him in a manger. How happy Mary and Joseph were to welcome God's Son into their family!

Solo: *Sing "You're a Gift, Baby Jesus," page 39.*

Narrator: That night, in the fields outside of Bethlehem, some shepherds were watching their sheep. They were amazed and frightened when some angels appeared to them.

Duet: *Sing "'Fear Not,' Said the Angel," page 40.*

God Keeps His Promises
continued

Narrator: What amazing and wonderful news! The shepherds just couldn't stay on the hillside any longer. They must go to Bethlehem and see if this was really true. They quickly left their sheep and went searching for the newborn Messiah. The angel was absolutely right! They found God's Son, the Lord Jesus, sleeping in a manger. They bowed down and worshipped this holy Son of God. Indeed, there never was a night like this before or since!

All: *Sing "Never a Night Like This," page 41.*

Narrator: After the shepherds had seen baby Jesus, they told everyone the wonderful news that God had kept His promise to send the Savior.

Far away in the east, some wise men, gazing at the sky the night Jesus was born, were surprised to see a very bright new star shining in the sky. They knew this meant that a new king was born in the land of Judea. They immediately made plans to go visit this newborn king.

Solo: *Sing "We Must Go," page 42.*

Narrator: The wise men were surprised when they arrived in Jerusalem to hear that King Herod didn't know about the birth of the new king. Herod asked the chief priests and scribes to tell him where Christ should be born. Reading in the book of Micah, they told Herod that God said He would be born in Bethlehem. Herod sent the wise men down the road to Bethlehem, telling them to let him know when they had found the promised Messiah. They were to come back and tell him so he could go and worship, too. The wise men went to Bethlehem where they found the child with Mary and Joseph—not in a manger now, but in a house. Bowing before the Son of God, they presented Him with gifts of gold, frankincense, and myrrh. Being warned by God in a dream that they should not return to Herod, the wise men went home another way.

God had kept all His promises concerning Jesus's birth. What about His promises that have still not been fulfilled? When Jesus went back to heaven, the disciples were amazed to hear an angel say that this same Jesus, who was taken up to heaven, would come again in the same way they had seen Him go. This has not happened yet, but because God cannot lie and always keeps His promises, we know beyond any doubt that Jesus will come back again. Will you be ready when He comes the second time?

All: *Sing "He Will Come Again," page 43.*

35   SS4861

You Can Always Count on God
by Dorothy Penrice

1. You can al-ways count on God for He al-ways keeps His pro-mi-ses. If He
2. List-en to Is-ai-ah's words as he pro-phe-sies of Je-sus' birth. Un-to

says that some-thing will hap-pen, it will be just as He says. When He
us a Child is born, un-to us a Son is given. And His

said He'd send the Sa-vior to this world in days of old, that is
name shall be called Won-der-ful, Coun-sel-or, the Prince of Peace. And the

Chorus

just what hap-pened in Beth-le-hem as the pro-phets had fore-told. You can
pro-mise was ful-filled that day in a sta-ble in Beth-le- hem.

al-ways count on God for His Word is e-ver true. If He

says it, He will do it. God can ne-ver lie to you.

SS4861

There's Room in the Stable

by Dorothy Penrice

1. There's no room to-night. There's no room to-night. There's no room to-night in
2. Kno-cking on each door, Jo-seph won-dered where, where they'd find a room in

Beth - le - hem. What will Jo - seph do? Where will Ma - ry go?
Beth - le - hem. Al - ways he did hear we've no room in here.

There's no room to-night in Beth - le - hem. But there's

Chorus

room in the sta - ble this Christ - mas night,

room with the an - i - mals here to - night.

This is God's plan for Je - sus' birth.

SS4861

There's Room in the Stable
continued

This is the night He will come to earth.

No roy - al pa - lace or king - ly crown,

no love - ly bed made of soft - est down.

But just a man - ger bed what a sight! Yes there's

room in the sta - ble to - night.

38

SS4861

You're a Gift, Baby Jesus
by Dorothy Penrice

You're a Gift, Ba - by Je - sus, gi - ven by our Heav'n - ly
Tho' our home's not a man - sion, but the home of a

Fa - ther with joy we wel - come You to - night. You have
car - pen - ter, You will find there's love and peace in it, for we

come, the pro - mised Sa - vior. Great is our re - spon - si
serve our Heav'n - ly Fa - ther. We're a - mazed that we were

bil - i - ty to care for God's own Son. We will
cho - sen in God's e - ter - nal plan to pro -

do our best, do it will - ing - ly. May Your per - fect will be done.
vide a home for Mes - si - ah. You are God, yet Son of Man.

SS4861

"Fear Not," Said the Angel

by Dorothy Penrice

"Fear not," said the an - gel, "Good ti - dings I bring. The
The shep - herds could hard - ly be - lieve what they saw a

Sav - ior is born to - day. In Beth - le - hem's man - ger you'll
sky full of an - gels bright. They list - ened in won - der, their

find Him, 'tis true. He's God's Gift on this Christ - mas Day.
hearts filled with awe— what news on that won - der - ful night!

Chorus

"Glo - ry to God, glo - ry to God." Join with the an - gels to sing.

"Peace on the earth, good will to men." Sing praise to Je - sus the King.

SS4861

Never a Night Like This
by Dorothy Penrice

Never was there a night like this. Never
was there a sight like this. I - mag - ine hear-ing the
To think that God sent His
an - gel tell that Christ is born, oh glo - ri - ous
on - ly Son to pay the pen - al - ty for all our
Gos - pel! Quick - ly the shep - herds did make their way
sin. Gaz - ing in - to the dear Sav - ior's face,
to see where Je - sus lay. They found Him sleep - ing on
they mar - velled at God's grace. Here was the hope for the
bed of hay. Nev - er a night like this.
hu - man race.

41

SS4861

"We Must Go"
by Dorothy Penrice

1. Far in the east some wise men gaz-ing at the sky one night,
2. Oh what a great ex-cite-ment as the wise men left that night.

saw a ver-ry brill-i-ant star shin-ing in the sky so bright.
No guide had they to show them the way, just the star that shone so bright.

Chorus

We must go, we must go, we must go to find the King.

Tho' it be far, we know the star, it will lead us to the King.

We will take gifts to Him prec-ious gifts to Him we'll bring.

Ho-ly One sent from heav'n we must find this King.

SS4861

He Will Come Again
by Dorothy Penrice

1. When Je - sus went back to hea - ven, the an - gel said that
2. Ma - ny years peo - ple wait - ed for Him to come as God had

He would come a - gain. Can we count on this pro - mise that
prom - ised He would do. And Je - sus was born there in

He will come, or will we wait in vain?
Beth - le - hem and He'll re - turn, 'tis true.

Chorus

He will come a - gain, not as a Ba - by as He did to

Beth - le - hem. He will come with power and

maj - es - ty and ev' - ry knee shall bow be - fore Him.

43

SS4861

Gifts for Jesus

by Jacqueline Schiff

Characters: 10 children

Setting: baby Jesus lying in a manger

Props: doll dressed as baby Jesus; large paper heart; cutout of dove of peace; pocket-size Bible; stuffed lamb, cow, horse, pig, or other farm animals; a couple of smiley face stickers; miniature Christmas tree; cutouts of shining stars; birthday cake; toy rattles or infant squeeze toys; a small table

(At opening, children individually carry a gift to baby Jesus and sing "I Give to Baby Jesus" (below) to the tune of "We Wish You a Merry Christmas." When they finish singing their parts, they present their gifts to Jesus and move to the back of the stage.)

Child 1: *(taking center stage and singing)*
I give love to baby Jesus,
I give love to baby Jesus,
I give love to baby Jesus
On His happy birth year.
(Hugs Jesus and places a large paper heart in His manger, then moves to rear of stage.)

Child 2: *(taking center stage and singing)*
I give peace to baby Jesus,
I give peace to baby Jesus,
I give peace to baby Jesus
On His happy birth year.
(Places a cutout of dove of peace in Jesus' manger, then moves to rear of stage.)

Child 3: *(taking center stage and singing)*
I give faith to baby Jesus,
I give faith to baby Jesus,
I give faith to baby Jesus
On His happy birth year.
(Places a Bible inside Jesus' manger, then moves to rear of stage.)

Child 4: *(taking center stage and singing)*
I bring friends for baby Jesus,
I bring friends for baby Jesus,
I bring friends for baby Jesus
On His happy birth year.
(Joins hands with Children 5 and 6 and leads them to Jesus' manger; then Child 4 moves to rear of stage.)

Child 5: *(kneeling over manger and singing)*
I bring pets for baby Jesus,
I bring pets for baby Jesus,
I bring pets for baby Jesus
On His happy birth year.
(Places a few stuffed animals in the manger, then moves to rear of stage.)

Child 6: *(kneeling over manger and singing)*
I give smiles to baby Jesus,
I give smiles to baby Jesus,
I give smiles to baby Jesus
On His happy birth year.
(Smiles at Jesus while placing smiley face stickers in the manger, then moves to rear of stage.)

Child 7: (taking center stage and singing)
I give toys to baby Jesus,
I give toys to baby Jesus,
I give toys to baby Jesus
On His happy birth year.
(Places infant toys inside Jesus' manger,
then moves to rear of stage.)

Child 8: (taking center stage and singing)
I give evergreen to Jesus,
I give evergreen to Jesus,
I give evergreen to Jesus
On His happy birth year.
(Places small Christmas tree beside Jesus' manger,
then moves to rear of stage.)

Child 9: (taking center stage and singing)
I give shining stars to Jesus,
I give shining stars to Jesus,
I give shining stars to Jesus
On His happy birth year.
(Places cutout stars in Jesus' manger,
then moves to rear of stage.)

Child 10: (taking center stage and singing)
I sing "Happy Birthday, Jesus,"
I sing "Happy Birthday, Jesus,"
I sing "Happy Birthday, Jesus,"
For Christmas is here.
(Places birthday cake on table beside the manger,
then moves to rear of stage.)

(All children take center stage and sing together beside manger.)

All: Good tidings we bring
To you, little child.
We wish you a Happy Birthday!
We're so happy You're here!

(Chorus)
We wish you a Happy Birthday,
We wish you a Happy Birthday,
We wish you a Happy Birthday,
Baby Jesus, You're dear!

(One at a time, each child kneels at the manger, hugs
the figure of baby Jesus, then exits the stage.)

When Jesus Was Born in Bethlehem

by Edith E. Cutting

Characters: narrator, chorus, Joseph, Mary, angels, shepherds

Setting: hut or cave enclosing manger filled with hay, at back of stage; Choir is offstage.

Props: box filled with hay for manger, spotlight or flashlight, baby wrapped in a blanket

Narrator: *(goes to stable)* This is the stable where Jesus was born in Bethlehem. *(touches manger)* This is the manger that stood in the stable where Jesus was born in Bethlehem. *(touches hay)* This is the hay that lay in the manger that stood in the stable where Jesus was born in Bethlehem.

Choir: *Sings "Away in a Manger"*

(Joseph enters.)

Narrator: *(pointing to him)* This is Joseph who led the donkey that came to the hay that lay in the manger that stood in the stable where Jesus was born in Bethlehem.

This is the donkey that came to the hay that lay in the manger that stood in the stable where Jesus was born in Bethlehem. *(Donkey from a life-size nativity set may be drawn onto stage, or if not available, action may go directly to Mary.)*

(Mary enters. Narrator touches her arm.) This is Mary who rode on the donkey that came to the hay that lay in the manger that stood in the stable where Jesus was born in Bethlehem.

Choir: *Sings "Silent Night"*

(Children wearing angel costumes appear at the left side of the stage opposite the narrator.)

Narrator: *(pointing)* These are the angels that told the shepherds that they should go to the manger that stood in the stable where Jesus was born in Bethlehem.

Choir: *Sings "It Came Upon a Midnight Clear"*

When Jesus Was Born in Bethlehem continued

(Angels leave stage as shepherds dressed in Biblical costumes come in at side, opposite narrator, and go to the stable where Jesus was born in Bethlehem.)

Choir: *Sings "The First Noel"*

(Spotlight or flashlight shines on doll in the manger.)

Narrator: *(standing by manger)* This is the baby that lay on the hay that filled the manger that stood in the stable where Jesus was born in Bethlehem.

(Angels come back in and join choir in singing "Infant Holy, Infant Lowly," while narrator, shepherds, Mary, and Joseph kneel by the manger.)

Narrator: *(stands and faces audience)* This is the story that lifts our hearts that we give to Jesus when we remember the baby that lay on the hay that filled the manger that stood in the stable where Jesus was born in Bethlehem.

Let us all join in singing "O Little Town of Bethlehem."

(Angels, shepherds, Mary, Joseph, and narrator lead the audience in singing with the choir.)

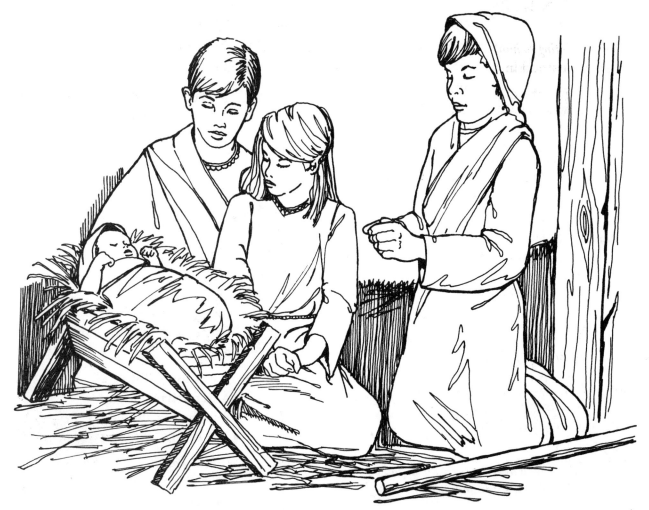

The Star of Jesus
by Edith E. Cutting

Characters: star, 3 wise men (dressed in colorful robes), Mary, Joseph, Jesus (about 2 years old)

Setting: mountains with Mary, Joseph, and Jesus hidden behind a screen

Props: a slender pole with a large gold star at its tip; steps (mountains); screen to hide Mary, Joseph, and Jesus

(A child enters carrying the star. Child comes to front-center and speaks.)

Star: I am the star,
The brightest shining star,
That leads people to Jesus
Wherever they are.

(Three children come onto stage as wise men. One comes close to the star and speaks.)

**First
Wise Man:** We are the wise men
Who studied the star.
We followed it always—
No matter how far.

(Star leads the others across the stage, up and down over the mountains; then all lift robes as if crossing river.)

Star: I led them through deserts
And mountains afar,
Till over the Jordan
They followed the star.

(Three wise men cluster, with second one pointing to the star and speaking.)

**Second
Wise Man:** No matter what happened,
We let nothing bar
Our planning to follow
This wonderful star.

(Third wise man holds out arms to indicate different directions. Unseen stagehand sets screen aside to show Mary, Joseph, and Jesus.)

**Third
Wise Man:** We came different ways
From countries afar,
To find the child Jesus
By Bethlehem's star.

(Manger is again screened; star comes to front of stage to speak. Star leads wise men off stage.)

Star: It was long, long ago,
And farther than far,
But Jesus is always
The bright leading star.

(Choir may sing "We Three Kings" or "There's a Star in the Sky" as children leave the stage.)

SS4861